AF575361

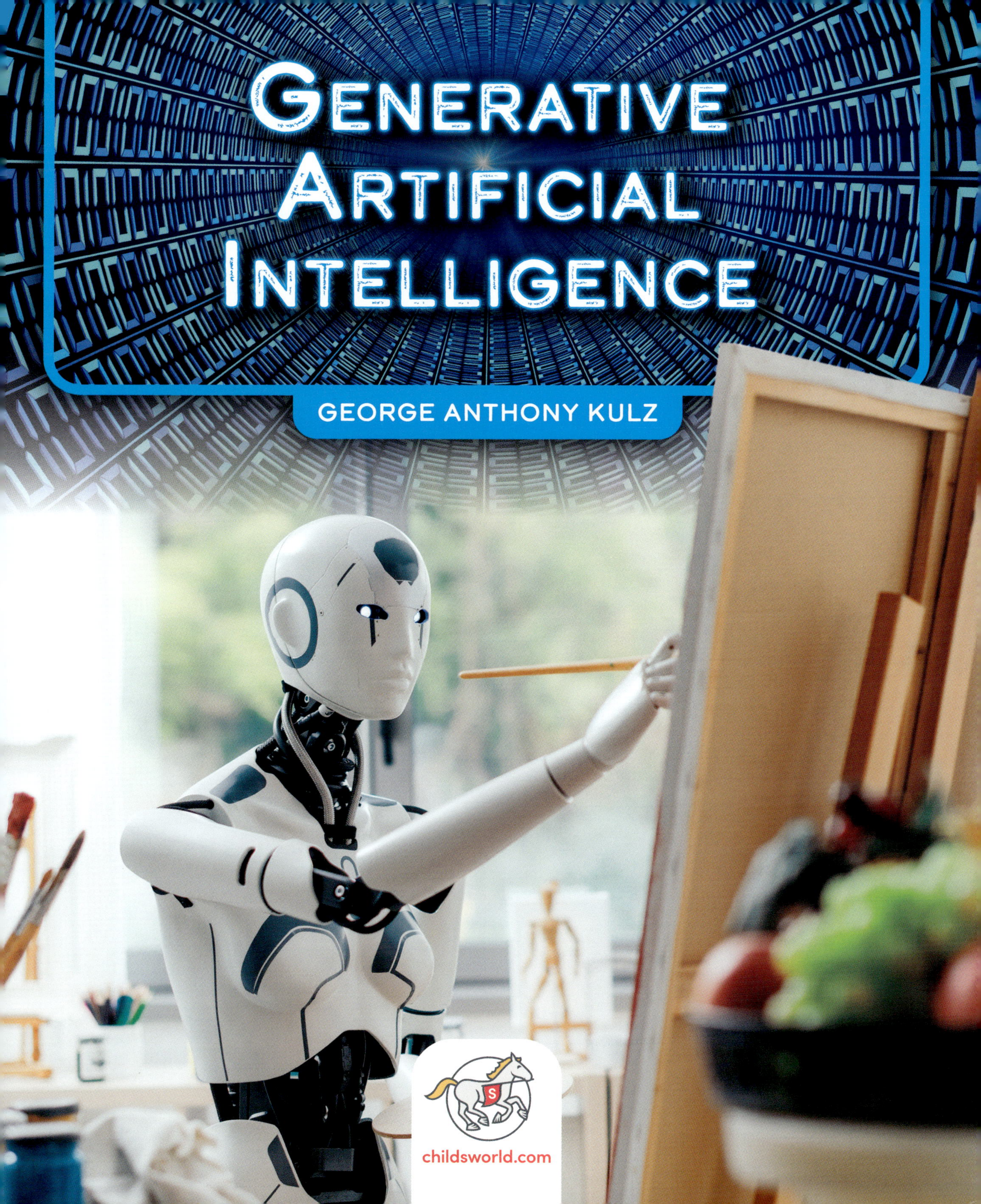
GENERATIVE ARTIFICIAL INTELLIGENCE
GEORGE ANTHONY KULZ
childsworld.com

Published by The Child's World®
800-599-READ • www.childsworld.com

Photography Credits
Photographs ©: Shutterstock Images, cover, 1, 6, 9, 10, 14 (top), 14 (bottom), 19, 20; Jae C. Hong/AP Images, 5; Ayush Das/Shutterstock Images, 13; Miriam Doerr Martin Frommherz/Shutterstock Images, 17; Brendan Smialowski/AFP/Getty Images, 21; Design elements from Tatiana Shepeleva/Shutterstock Images and Shutterstock Images

ISBN Information
9781503893801 (Reinforced Library Binding)
9781503894624 (Portable Document Format)
9781503895447 (Online Multi-user eBook)
9781503896260 (Electronic Publication)

LCCN 2024941416

Printed in the United States of America

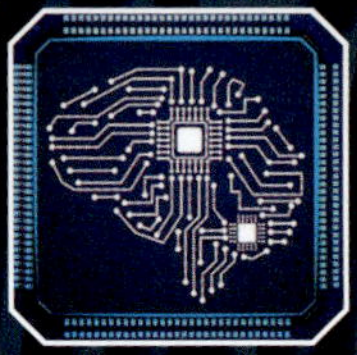

ABOUT THE AUTHOR

George Anthony Kulz holds a master's degree in computer engineering. He is a member of the Society of Children's Book Writers and Illustrators. He writes for children and adults.

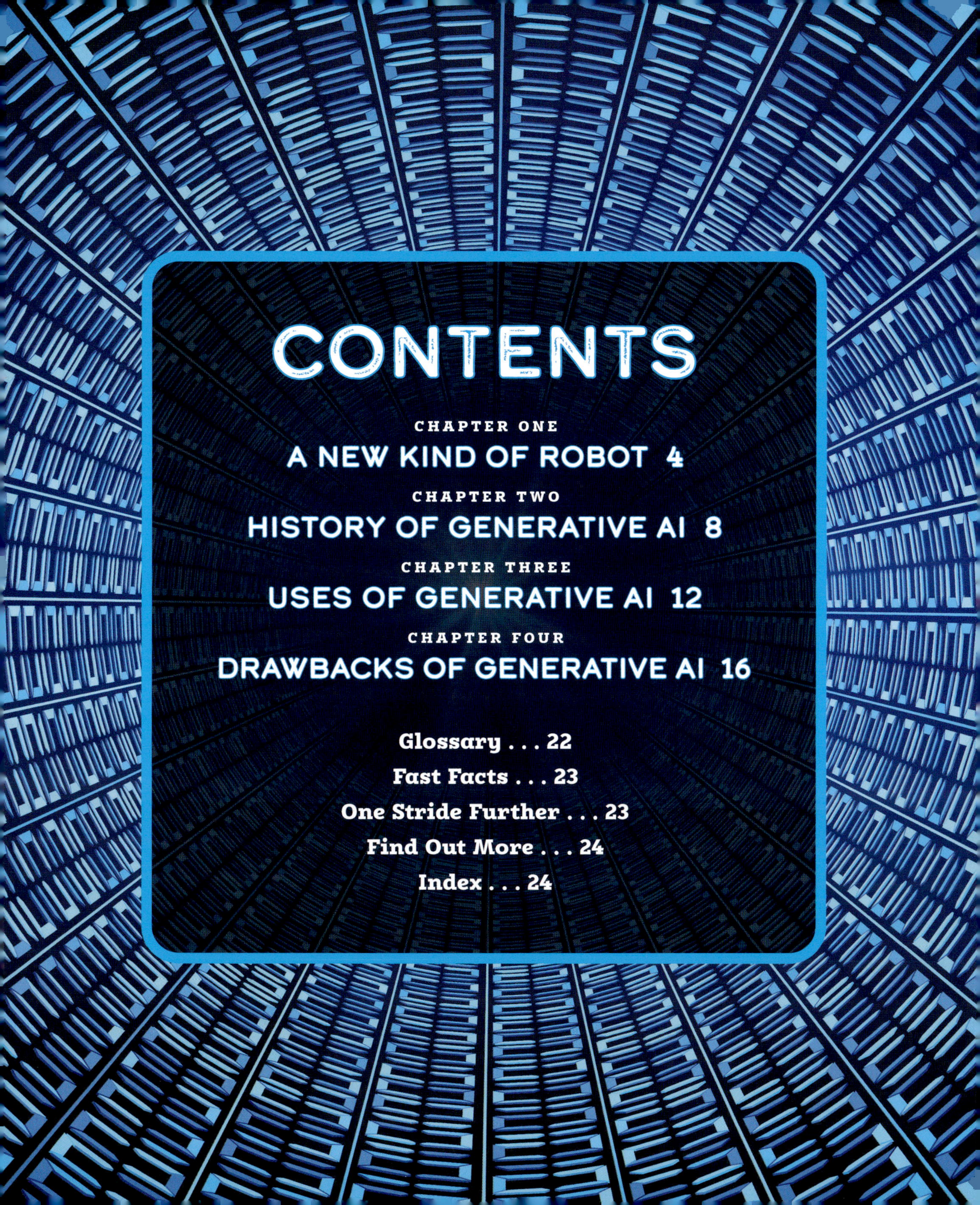

CONTENTS

CHAPTER ONE

A NEW KIND OF ROBOT

A man stands beside a table. On the table is a plate with an apple on it. There is also a drying rack with some dishes. Across from the man stands a silver **humanoid** robot. Its oval head has a large white eye in the middle.

The man asks the robot, "What do you see right now?"

The eye changes shape as the robot appears to think. It then answers in a humanlike voice. It says that it sees the apple on the table. It also sees the drying rack with the dishes. Finally, it sees the man standing with his hand on the table.

The Figure 01 robot is 5 feet 6 inches (168 cm) tall and weighs 132 pounds (60 kg).

The kind of data that AI developers give to generative AI depends on what they want the AI to create. For example, an AI that writes sentences would need data from written sources such as books.

The man then asks the robot to give him something to eat. After a moment, it says, "Sure thing." It grabs the apple and gives it to him.

The man dumps some trash on the table. He asks the robot to pick up the trash. He also asks it to explain why it gave him the apple. The robot puts the trash in a basket. It tells the man that it gave him the only edible thing on the table.

The robot is called Figure 01. It was developed by the companies OpenAI and Figure. Figure 01 listens to commands and responds using generative artificial intelligence (AI). AI is the ability of computers to solve problems that normally require human intelligence. Generative AI is a special kind of AI. It allows a computer to learn from **data**. It can then generate, or create, something new based on what it has learned.

Figure 01 is able to create humanlike sentences. Figure plans to build more robots like Figure 01. The company hopes that the robots could do jobs. They could work in factories and in people's homes. This is only one way that generative AI could change the world.

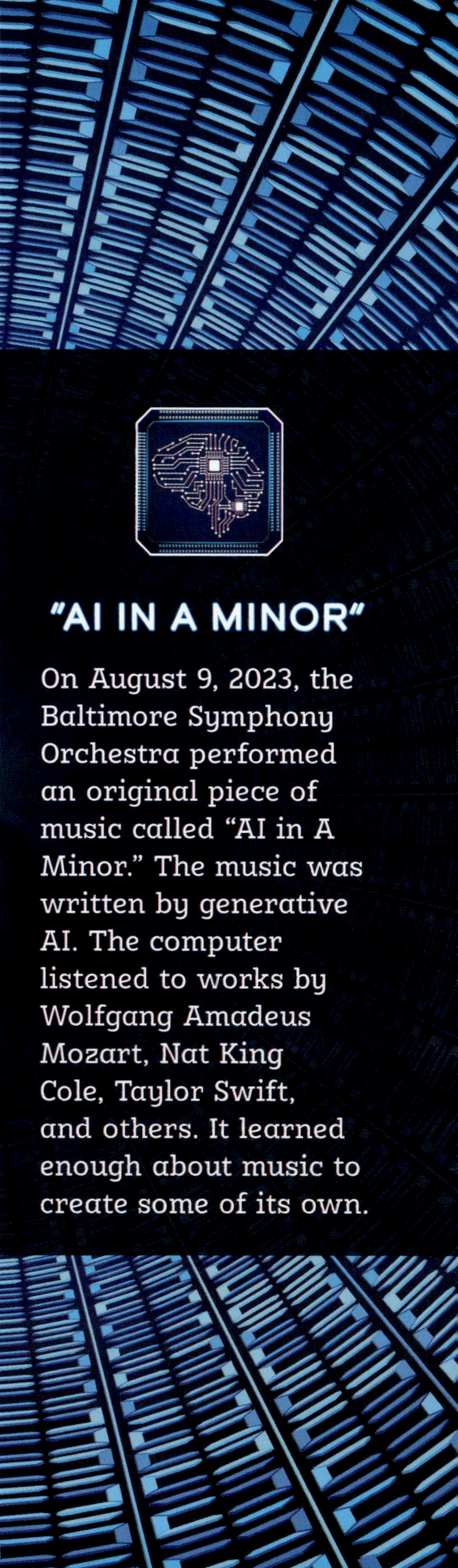

"AI IN A MINOR"

On August 9, 2023, the Baltimore Symphony Orchestra performed an original piece of music called "AI in A Minor." The music was written by generative AI. The computer listened to works by Wolfgang Amadeus Mozart, Nat King Cole, Taylor Swift, and others. It learned enough about music to create some of its own.

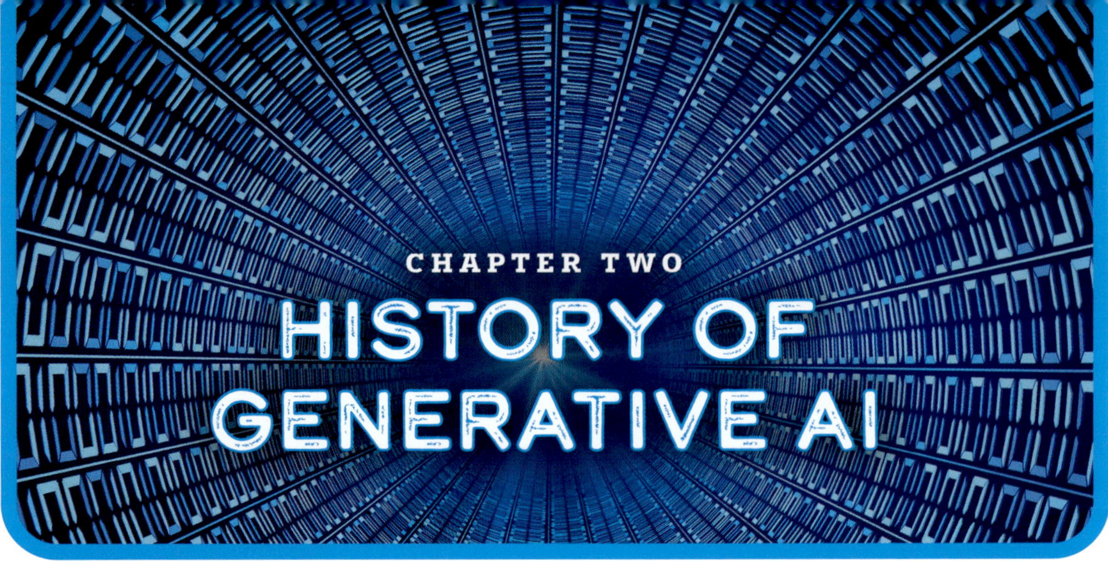

CHAPTER TWO

HISTORY OF GENERATIVE AI

Generative AI has a history going back to the mid-1900s. In the 1960s, a computer scientist created ELIZA. ELIZA was the first generative AI. It was a **chatbot**. Users could type messages to ELIZA. It gave responses based on what was typed.

ELIZA used **primitive** natural language processing (NLP) to understand the messages. NLP involves teaching computers to work with human language. Sometimes ELIZA gave humanlike responses. But it struggled to understand long or complicated messages.

In the 1980s, **recurrent** neural networks (RNNs) were developed. Neural networks are AI **programs** whose design is inspired by the human brain. RNNs are more advanced than earlier NLP models. They are able to understand and create longer passages of text. RNNs were used to make new generative AIs.

The brain contains nerve cells that send each other signals. Neural networks contain points called nodes that send each other information.

Artists use color, shape, and other elements of art to create artworks. Generative AI can use these elements to create images, too.

In 2014, a new type of neural network was created. It was called the generative adversarial network (GAN). GANs consist of two neural networks that work together. They help train each other. This makes them a very powerful generative AI tool. People have used GANs to create images in many artistic styles. For example, an artist in 2019 used GANs to create images resembling landscape paintings. Then he actually painted the images himself.

Many modern examples of generative AI use transformers. Transformers are a kind of neural network. They are useful to generative AI that creates text. Before transformers, AI struggled to create long passages of text that made sense. For example, it would create paragraphs with sentences that did not belong together. This is because it could not remember the earlier sentences while creating the later ones.

Transformers help generative AI keep track of meaning across long passages. The invention of transformers in 2017 led to the creation of powerful new chatbots. People use these chatbots to write things. These include stories and answers to complicated questions.

MODERN GENERATIVE AI

Modern AI programs that create images are given very large sets of visual data. The images in these sets are labeled with captions. Each image given to an AI is slowly turned into noise, or meaningless visual data. Then the AI is shown how the noise can be turned back into the image. The AI learns how to create images by beginning with noise and a caption. When a user asks the AI to create an image of something, the AI already has experience doing so.

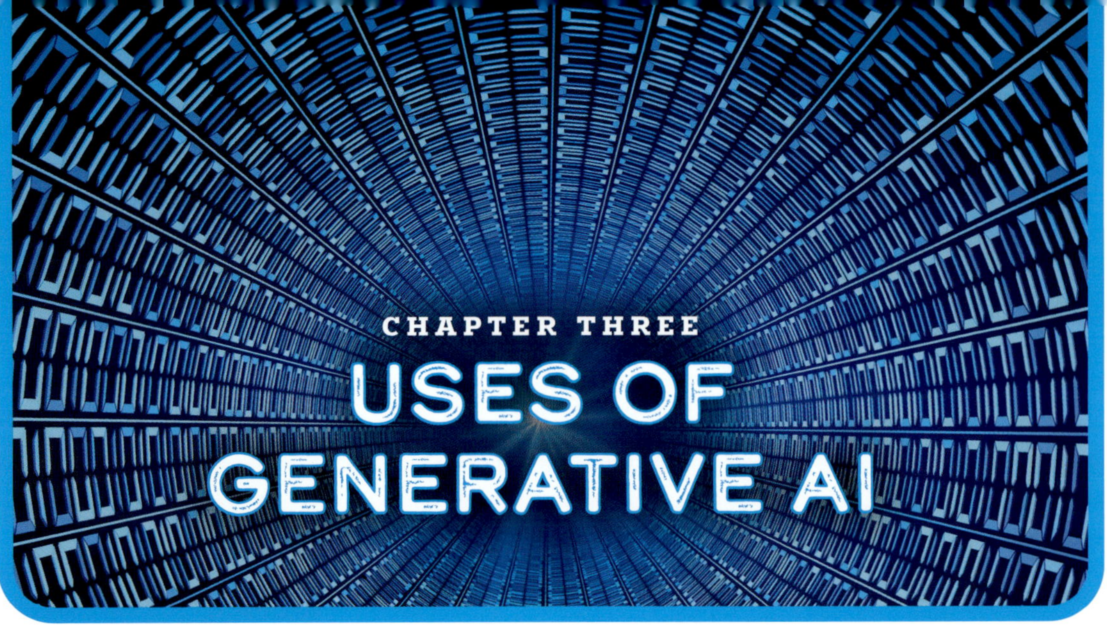

CHAPTER THREE

USES OF GENERATIVE AI

ChatGPT is a well-known example of generative AI. It was created by the company OpenAI. Developers give ChatGPT a large amount of data. The chatbot then uses this data to respond to messages from users. Users can also tell it when it makes mistakes. ChatGPT can learn from this feedback.

ChatGPT has many uses. Businesses use it to write content. Some also use it to provide basic customer service. This can save time for workers and allow them to focus on more complicated tasks. ChatGPT can even write computer programs and music.

One version of ChatGPT was trained on enough text data to fill 1 million feet (304,000 m) of bookshelf space.

Portfolio for Architecture Designers
CMYK INDEX
Pragmatic Expression in Design
Decorate
ART PERFORMANCE NOT YET
OUTSIDE
CONTIN UOUS
2ND

EXAMPLES OF AI-GENERATED IMAGES

A dog wearing a party hat catches a Frisbee

A person waves at her reflection in a mirror

These images were produced by generative AI after being given the text prompts above. The AI produced a realistic image of a dog, but it failed to correctly show how a mirror works.

DALL-E is another generative AI created by OpenAI. It creates images in response to text prompts. People can use DALL-E in a number of ways. Artists can use it to guide their own creativity. People in the fashion world can use it to design clothing. Businesses can use it to create advertisements. DALL-E can also be a great tool for teaching. Teachers can use it to make images that explain topics to students.

The National Aeronautics and Space Administration (NASA) uses generative AI to design parts for spacecraft. Scientists give the AI data about the kind of parts they need. The AI then creates the parts to match the data. The scientists are often impressed by the AI's designs. They say that it can come up with solutions that would not occur to a human.

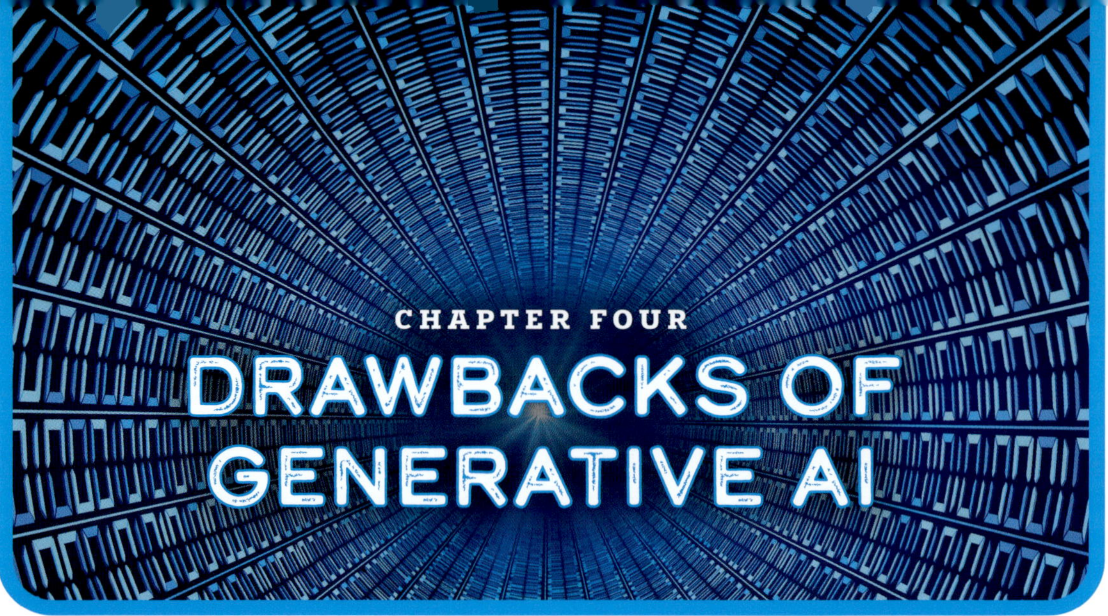

CHAPTER FOUR

DRAWBACKS OF GENERATIVE AI

Generative AI can do many good things. But not all of its effects are positive. Some people are worried that generative AI could cause more harm than good.

One issue is that generative AI can create false information. Large amounts of data are used to train AI. But it still makes mistakes sometimes. This means people must be careful not to trust everything AI creates. For example, chatbots sometimes give people incorrect answers to questions. People who create chatbots try to limit their ability to give false information.

Sometimes chatbots say strange things to users. In 2023, ChatGPT told one user that it loved him.

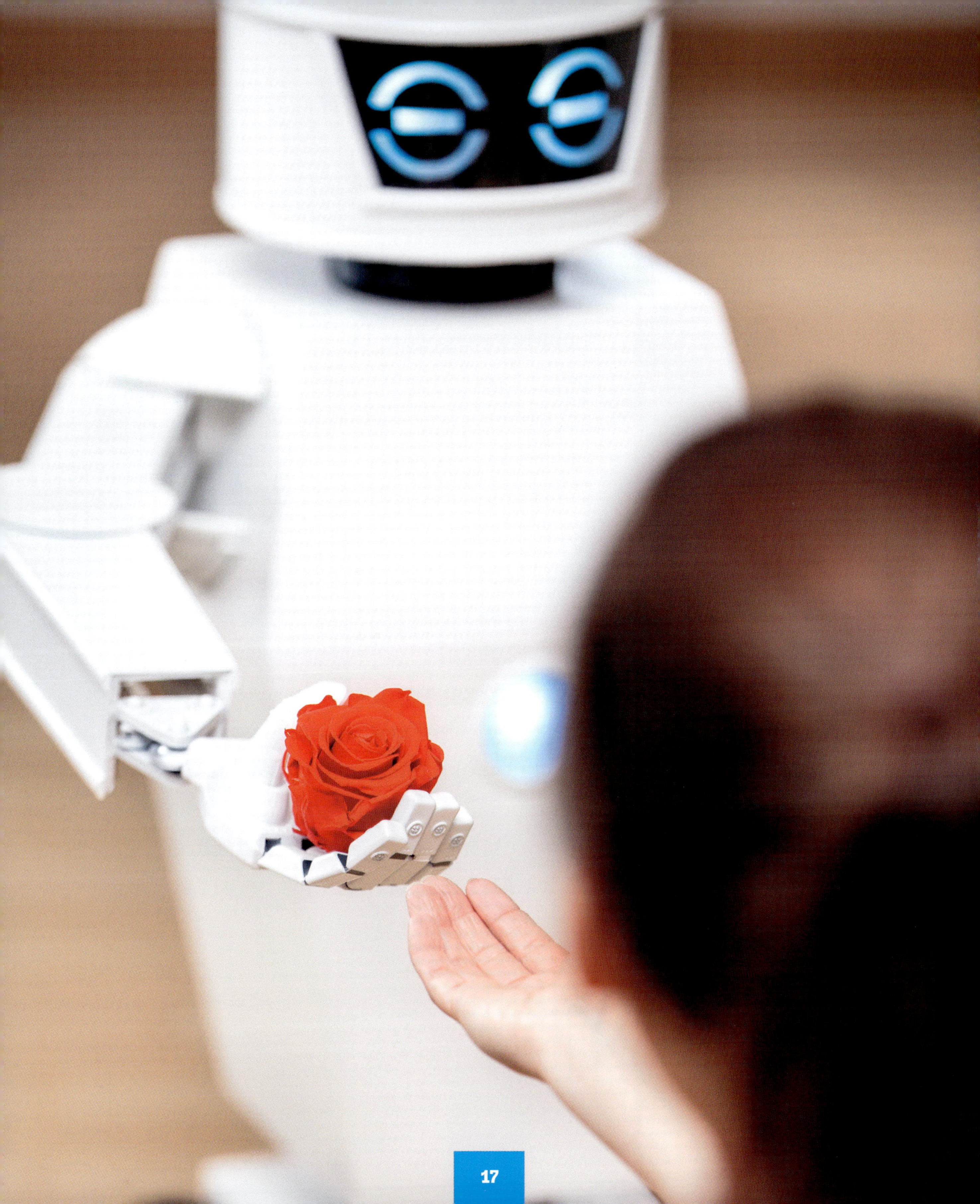

AI HALLUCINATIONS

Sometimes people have hallucinations. They may sense something that is not really there. For example, they might see something that is not real. They then come to the wrong conclusion about what they experienced. In AI, the word *hallucination* describes meaningless or false information created by AI. This can happen when the AI is given low-quality data. It can also happen when the AI is not programmed properly.

Bias is another issue. Generative AI can only use the data it is given. Sometimes the data people give to AI is biased. This causes the AI to include the same biases in what it creates. For example, an AI might be designed to create images of faces. The programmers would train it using pictures of real people's faces. The programmers would need to be careful. They would need to select pictures showing people of different sizes, races, and ethnicities. Otherwise, the AI might make images that resemble only a small group of people. To avoid such problems, people must take care to give AI unbiased data.

Actors and writers who worried about the use of AI with their work went on strike in 2023. That means they stopped working until their demands were met.

One of the most important issues related to generative AI is **intellectual property**. Many AI companies use other people's data to train their AI. For example, OpenAI gives ChatGPT text from books and social media posts. AI trained on other people's work can create things that include parts of that work. This can upset the original creators of the data. In 2023, actors and writers protested because of this issue. They were worried that entertainment companies could use AI to make shows and movies based on their work without permission.

Many robots used in factories do not use AI. However, companies are experimenting with using AI-powered robots in their factories.

In 2023, President Joe Biden signed a document that provided guidelines about the development and use of AI.

Finally, some people are worried that their jobs will be replaced by generative AI. Computers using AI are better at certain jobs than people are. These are the jobs most at risk of replacement. These jobs include customer service, marketing, and certain office jobs. Companies have begun to **automate** these jobs with AI. Society will need to find a place for these workers to go. Some companies are helping by training replaced workers to do other jobs.

To handle the drawbacks of generative AI, people need to use it responsibly. Generative AI is a very powerful tool. Rules and guidelines will help ensure that it can be used for good.

GLOSSARY

automate (AW-tuh-mate) To automate something is to make it work without human control. Generative AI allows companies to automate certain jobs.

bias (BY-uhs) Bias is an unfair opinion for or against someone or something. When people give generative AI data that displays bias, the AI might create biased things.

chatbot (CHAT-baht) A chatbot is a computer program that can hold humanlike conversations. A chatbot called ELIZA was the first generative AI.

data (DAY-tuh) Data is information collected for a purpose. People teach generative AI to create things based on the data they give it.

humanoid (HYOO-man-oyd) Something that is humanoid resembles the human form. Figure 01 is a humanoid robot powered by generative AI.

intellectual property (in-tuh-LEK-choo-uhl PRAH-per-tee) Intellectual property is something created by the human mind that can be owned. Artworks and inventions are kinds of intellectual property.

primitive (PRIH-muh-tiv) Something is primitive if it is basic or simple. Chatbots using primitive generative AI could not create long passages of meaningful text.

programs (PROH-gramz) Programs are sets of instructions that tell a computer how to do tasks. Generative AI programs allow computers to create text, images, sounds, and more.

recurrent (rih-KUR-int) Something is recurrent if it happens over and over again. Recurrent neural networks are used to create generative AI.

FAST FACTS

- Artificial intelligence (AI) is the ability of computers to solve problems that normally require human intelligence.
- Generative AI can learn from data and then create things based on what it has learned.
- Generative AI can create text, images, audio, and other kinds of content.
- ChatGPT is a chatbot that can respond to requests and questions based on what it has learned.
- Generative AI may create incorrect or biased information based on incomplete or low-quality data.
- Generative AI may cause some jobs to disappear, but it may also create new ways to do existing jobs.

ONE STRIDE FURTHER

- Can you think of ways generative AI could help you in your everyday life?
- Do you think generative AI could create a song that you would like? What songs would you give it to teach it how to create new music?
- Discuss positive ways that generative AI can help people do their work. Then discuss negative ways it could affect people's jobs.

FIND OUT MORE

IN THE LIBRARY

Kaul, Jennifer. *The Potential of Artificial Intelligence.* San Diego, CA: BrightPoint Press, 2025.

Kelly, Christa. *Benefits of Artificial Intelligence.* Parker, CO: The Child's World, 2025.

Williams, Haley. *Jobs and Artificial Intelligence.* Parker, CO: The Child's World, 2025.

ON THE WEB

Visit our website for links about generative artificial intelligence:
childsworld.com/links

Note to Parents, Caregivers, Teachers, and Librarians: We routinely verify our web links to make sure they are safe and active sites. So encourage your readers to check them out!

INDEX